Show, Don't Tell

By

Roseanne Dowell

ISBN: -13:978-1508633358

PUBLISHED BY:
R&R Publishing.

Copyright 2015 by Roseanne Dowell

Lesson 1- Avoiding Adverbs –.

Writing without adverbs? Really? Yes, really. Everything you've learned in English class about describing with adverbs, forget it.

Then how do we describe people, tone of voice, or scenery? Some writers think adverbs are the only way to add description to a story.

Wrong – the use and over use of adverbs distracts from your story. It puts YOU, the AUTHOR, in the story. And we never (one of the few nevers in writing) want the author in the story. We want the reader to live the story.

There are better ways to add description. Let's take this sentence for example: Roy walked leisurely down the street. - Okay you, the author, just TOLD us how Roy walked – you interfered with the story. How much better if you would have showed us how Roy walked –

Example:
Roy strolled down the street. Notice how just changing the verb and taking out the adverb shows us how Roy walked.

Roy is not in a hurry -strolled implies leisurely without the author saying so. But let's take it one step farther, the author can show more.

Roy breathed in the spring air. He loved this time of year with the trees budding, especially the smell of fresh cut grass. He stopped and looked at the sky, loved the way the sun glistened off the trees.

Now the author hasn't even told us that Roy strolled. We know he's not in a hurry because he notices everything around him. People in a hurry don't take the time to notice the buds on the trees. They wouldn't stop to look at the sky. The author is showing us something about Roy besides the fact that he's not in a hurry. Roy loves spring and nature. Some people wouldn't notice the buds on the trees, even when they're not in a hurry. People react in different ways to show us they aren't in a hurry. Maybe they'd lollygag along, watching the traffic, or kids playing. That shows us something different about them. People have different interests and see different things and so should our characters.

Adverbs can never replace strong verbs. As in the above example, strolled is a much stronger verb then walked in showing us how someone went on his way. Yet, there was still a better way to show without telling us he strolled. It shows Roy doing something and tells us something about him.

We always want to show our characters. If Roy was a grumpy old man, he wouldn't have noticed the same things Roy, the nature lover, noticed. More than likely, the grumpy old man would notice something negative, litter on the street or kids yelling while they play, things that annoy him.

Think about your character before you write. Know them inside out. Know everything about them, their hobbies, occupation, even their favorite color. Make a character worksheet, listing, not just his physical characteristics, but his occupation, hobbies, favorite things. I've shown example after this lesson.

Adverbs combined with strong verbs – He ran quickly – are repetitive. We already know he ran, that tells us he's moving fast, why repeat it. I know if someone is running, they're moving quickly. The adverb has the same meaning as the verb. By adding the adverb we weaken the verb and the sentence, and it shows us nothing.

Avoid the use of adverbs whenever possible. When you feel tempted to add an adverb, stop and think about what you want the reader to know. Is there another way to say it? Usually there is.

Adverbs to describe how someone speaks are also interfering.

Example: "Stop, just stop," John shouted angrily.

Well, I don't know about you but if someone is shouting that usually means he's angry or upset.

Why not show us the anger. "Stop! Just stop." John slammed a cupboard door.

Now that shows us he's angry much better than the adverb angrily? And we didn't have to use the tag line he shouted. We can say, he shouted and slammed the cupboard door, but does that reinforce the anger? Not really. The action works better alone.

Now don't get me wrong – there are places to use adverbs, but the key is to use them sparingly. Readers want detail, they want to see, hear, and smell the story. They don't want someone to tell them what happened. They want to feel the anger, sadness, happiness, laughter, and tears. Readers want to experience our character's emotion. Characters who display emotion are strong characters. And readers remember them. They become real, believable. And if we have believable characters, readers will remember us.

So next time you write, she hurried quickly down the street, STOP!! Reread what you just wrote. Do you really want to repeat that she was in a hurry? Hurried already implies she was going quickly.

And next time you write – "I can't do this anymore," John said sadly. Rethink it – is there a better way to show John sad? "I can't do this anymore." John wiped the tears from his eyes. Notice I didn't say John said as he wiped the tears. You can also eliminate the he said/she said tags and insert an action tag that shows us more of what's happening. By saying John said sadly, we know John is sad – but we don't know he's crying. In fact we don't know anything about John.

We add so much more to the story by eliminating needless adverbs. We all enjoy reading strong stories, why not write them.

Practice Assignment:
 Change the adverbs in the story below to strong verbs and thus change the whole tone of the story, showing instead of telling. You can expand on it if you wish.
You can change the sentence structure if you want, but stick to the same story elements.

John walked hurriedly. He thought about his argument with Sarah. Sarah sure had yelled loud enough. He had made her so mad. He never heard her yell so loudly.

He remembered her words. "How could you do something so stupid, John?" she yelled loudly. Then she threw the ring angrily across the room.

He felt in his pocket and took out the ring. He couldn't believe she threw it across the room. She was mad because he put it on the charge account.

"I don't need a ring that big," she cried angrily. Slowly she had turned and left him standing alone.

He was on his way to take the ring back. He went into the store cautiously. He didn't know how he was going to explain this.

"Excuse me," he said hesitantly.

The man behind the counter looked up. "Can I help you?"

"I, uh, yes, I bought this ring yesterday and um." John coughed softly to cover up his embarrassment.

"I understand," the man behind the counter said sympathetically. "She doesn't want to get married right now. That's okay we'll take the ring back."

John gave the man his receipt. He sighed loudly, relieved. At least he wouldn't have a big bill now. He looked at cheaper rings but decided to bring Sarah in to pick out one she'd like. Hopefully she would agree.

He left the store and walked quickly home. He wanted to find Sarah and tell her the good news. Now he didn't have the big bill and she'd have to forgive him.

"Sarah, guess what. I took the ring back and they took it off my bill." John said laughingly.

"That's great, John. I feel much better now. We can't start our marriage off with a big bill like that," Sarah said happily.

John placed his hand on her back gently and kissed her cheek. "Would you come with me to pick out your ring?" he asked slowly.

Sarah looked at him lovingly. "Sure, John, but you know it's not going to be as big as the one you picked out. I want you to buy something you can afford." She rubbed her finger along his cheek tenderly. "I didn't mean to get so angry at you. I just knew you over extended yourself and I didn't want our marriage to be bogged down with that kind of expense. We have to save every penny for our wedding.

John let out a big sigh of relief. He knew Sarah was right. He knew she'd make a good wife. She watched her money frugally and wouldn't spend wastefully. "I love you, Sarah McCoy." He said affectionately.

"I love you, too, John Stewart." Sarah smiled dreamily.

Below is the character worksheet I use. I use them for all the main characters in my story.

CHARACTER WORKSHEET

1. Name – Nickname
2. Age – Birthday
3. General info – Hair color, eyes; height; weight
4. Favorites – color, sport; food
5. Hobbies
6. What do you think of when you first see him/her – phrase or word to describe. Thin fit, tall, short, muscular, flabby
7. First physical impression. Sloppy distinguished, snobby; sophisticated
8. What do you sense from his/her personality? Shy;confident;bold; loud
9. What type of clothes does he/she wear at work? At home?
10. What is his/her voice like? Rough, raspy, soft, smooth, shrill, Is there an accent?
11. Where does he/she live? Why? His/her choice? Necessity?(job school)
12. Where was he/she born? Describe his/ her background. (family life etc.)
13. Who most influenced his/her life?
14. What's are his/her priorities? Daydreams, fantasies

15. What motivates him/her?
16. What are his/her conflicts? Does he/she settle them him/herself? Or does she have help?
17. What are his/her goals? How far would they go to achieve them?
18. What are his/her fears? Does it keep her/him from achieving their goals?
19. How important is it for him/her to win?
20. How does he/she react to children? Animals? How do you know?
21. How does he/she interact with others in the story?
22. How does he/she shape the plot
23. What are his/her undesirable characteristics? Faults? Quick tempered/impatient?
24. What are his/her quirks? Special talents?
25. What does he/she do for a living?
26. Why does the reader care what happens to him/.her?

Lesson 2 - Actions Speak Louder than Words

Body language and facial expressions play a large part in our daily conversation, they're natural reactions to what we speak and hear. Our characters should react the same way. If we forget these important elements, our dialogue will appear flat, boring, and our characters dull. Even setting plays a part in every day conversation.

Did you ever avoid someone's eyes – focus on a picture or a lamp - maybe even lowered your eyes or stared at the ceiling? We tend to focus on things other than the person speaking to us if we're uncomfortable with either the situation or the person.

We wave our hand, cross our arms, tap our foot, or raise our eyebrows to show impatience. Maybe we wrinkle our brow, scrunch up our nose, and let out a deep sigh when we're doubtful. We cross our leg, wiggle our foot, or tap our fingers when we're nervous. All of these actions show something about our moods, our reactions to conversation, and even about us. We react differently when we're nervous, upset, irritated, happy, sad, scared, or doubtful. These actions show what dialogue, alone, cannot. Our characters need to do the same.

Teamed up with dialogue these expressive actions say more about our character, their setting, and their dialogue then the typical he said, she said and their counterparts -replied, asked, responded. These are unnecessary words, they do nothing to show, and usually tell, something we want to avoid. Also, other than said, they put the author into the story – something I've previously said we never want. Said, on the other hand, disappears into the story and most readers don't notice it.

Think of a strong dialogue scene as having three elements: words, visuals, and thoughts." Let's see how it works.

How often have we created dialogue like this?

"I can't believe you said that," he said.

"Why not, it's true," she replied.

"But, you didn't have to say it," he answered.

"No, I guess I didn't," she said.

We tag the dialogue with he said, she said so our readers do not get confused about who is speaking. We vary said with replied, answered, snapped or other similar words. The dialogue is boring. We know nothing about the characters. We can change he/she to Tom and Laura, but it won't change the dialogue. All we have are words. We can add adverbs to the tag lines to tell us what they're feeling as in the following example.

"I can't believe you said that," he said angrily.

Okay, now we know he's angry, but you, the author, told us that, not the character and we still have he said. Our characters are not showing us anything. And we already learned about the misuse of adverbs in lesson one. We know that doesn't work. It's telling, not showing. So what do we do?

Next step adding visuals. We add visuals by setting a scene - Tom and Laura sat in a restaurant. Sure, we can do that, but then the author's voice is back in the story. Remember, we want to stay out of the story as much as possible. We want the characters to set the scene.

Think about a conversation with your spouses or good friends. While they were speaking, you formed your answers in your mind. And you watched their face, noticed their body language at the same time. Maybe their body tensed, their jaw set, their brow furrowed or they frowned. Through their body language you knew they were upset or angry, happy, or sad. Other thoughts flowed through your mind. Maybe you were angry too or thought they were wrong. The interchange included words, body language, and your thoughts. Many things happened during that conversation.

Now, let's add some visuals and body language to our earlier conversation and see how it plays out.

"I can't believe you said that." Tom stared at her.

Laura looked at the waiter, avoiding the hurt look on Tom's face. "Why not, it's true." She watched him out of the corner of her eye.

Tom's jaw tightened. He picked up his cup, took a sip. "But you didn't have to say it."

"No, I guess I didn't."

Notice how we eliminated the he said, she said completely. Yet, we still know who is speaking. We can see and hear their emotion. Examine what the above exchange shows us, based on the criteria. We had the conversation in the first dialogue session and it showed us nothing but the speakers. In the example above, we added a visual and a scene, the restaurant.

We know this because she stared at a waiter and he picked up the cup. We've added tension with body language - His jaw tightened. We know she is our POV, because she sees the hurt. We see the scene and hear the words through her. We see her visually ignoring him, yet watching his reaction.

We vary the length and pace of the sentences to keep the reader's attention. Sometimes, as in the case of his last comment, it is more powerful not to add a visual or tag line. If we add visuals or tag lines to all dialogue, it becomes monotonous and boring and can even disrupt our story.

We now have two elements, words and visuals. Let's add the third, thoughts.

"I can't believe you said that." Tom stared at her.

She looked at the waiter, avoiding the hurt look on his face. "Why not, it's true." She watched him out of the corner of her eye. As usual, he was angry. This was getting tiring. He always had to be right.

His jaw tightened. He played with his cup. "But you didn't have to say it."

"No, I guess I didn't." She stood. She'd had enough. Glaring at him, she pulled some change from her purse and threw it on the table. It was always about him. She hurried out, before she said something she'd regret later.

We have completed the elements. We hear the characters voices and see their emotions. They've set the scene and their reaction to the words and we have her thoughts. Our characters have brought the scene to life, and you, the author did not tell us anything. Notice I didn't have internal thoughts. I paraphrased. More about that later.

Practice Assignment:

Change the story below adding the three elements described above, words, visuals and thoughts as shown in the examples. You decide who the POV is. Continue on with the story in your own words if you want.

Tony looked at Jenny. "What's the big news?" he asked.

"I just found out I'm accepted to Harvard," she said excitedly.

The light changed and Tony waited for the car in front of him to move. "That's great, Jenn," he said. "Why doesn't that idiot move?" He blew his horn and the car in front of him finally moved forward." "When do you start? And where does that leave us? Harvard's pretty far away," he said angrily.

"I don't have to be there until the end of August. We still have the whole summer."

Tony didn't answer. He dropped her off at home and kissed her cheek. "See you later," he said.

"Tony, I... it doesn't have to be the end of us. We can email, talk on the phone or instant message. And I'll come home for holidays. You can visit," Jenny said sadly. "We'll work it out. But this is a big opportunity for me."

"Yeah, I know." Tony said. "I'll see you later."

Lesson 3 – I Smell a Story

Did you ever notice that unless something smells especially good or particularly offensive, we tend to ignore it?

Because our sense of sight and hearing are dominant we tend to ignore every day smells. We see the trees, hear the traffic, and look into each other's eyes as we speak.

But we take our other senses, touch, taste, and smell for granted. We often ignore them. Oh sure, we feel, taste and smell, but not with a lot of awareness. While the smell of bacon makes our mouth water and we may say it smells good, or that it is making us hungry, we don't elaborate on it.

On the other hand if we smell something offensive, say a skunk, we go on and on about the distasteful odor. Same thing with taste. The bacon and egg taste good and we enjoy them, but we expect to enjoy them so we don't say much about them. On the other hand, the sour taste of vinegar or a lemon has us spitting and complaining about the acrid flavor.

The same applies to our sense of touch. We feel something soft or silky, it's comforting, and we might make an off-handed remark. But, if we burn, cut, or hurt ourselves, we complain and make a big deal about the pain.

All of these senses are important to us in our stories as sight and sound. We describe the setting, the background. But by using all of our senses we bring our stories to life. We can go from the real world we live in to a new world of make believe. Of course, we also need to make our story realistic. In both fiction and nonfiction, a richly described setting will pull your readers out of the real world of pressure and tension and into your world of make believe. So how then, can we ignore these senses in our descriptions?

We need to become more aware of these senses in our everyday world? Go outside, look around you - listen to the sounds. Now close your eyes. Inhale deeply, breath in the odors. What do you smell? The flowers, exhausts from cars, it depends where you are. You can do the same wherever you go. Walk into a department store at a mall. Inhale the scents. What do you smell, the lingering scent of someone's perfume or the perfume counter, if a smoker walks past you, you detect the odor of cigarette smoke. At a movie it will probably be the smell of popcorn. Restaurants have many smells, garlic, onions, rich sauces or maybe coffee. Remember these smells. Use them in your writing.

Next time you eat, savor the food. Hold it in your mouth, relish the experience and texture of bread and the slight aroma of yeast. Feel the surface of the tabletop or tablecloth. Ingrain them into your memory.

Use these senses in the story. Let us hear, see, feel, smell and taste the story. The story and characters will come alive through these senses. It's not enough to tell us what something looks like. SHOW US!! We want to feel it, smell it, and maybe even taste it. Readers won't notice that you included them, but they will notice if you omit them. Without them, your world will be flat, boring, and unrealistic.

No, you don't have to add them to every sentence or even every scene. Maybe your characters are in a situation where they don't notice smells or textures and there is nothing to taste. That's often true of tense scenes. If someone is attacking you, you certainly aren't going to notice the sweet smell of roses. On the other hand you might notice the offensive odor of his sweat. And you'll certainly feel the beads of perspiration on your own forehead or the taste the nausea building up from your throat to your mouth.

Other times we might be deep in thought and won't even notice our surroundings. That's fine, but make sure to include them when they are needed. If your characters walk into a restaurant, we want to know what they smell as well as what they see and hear. Too often, as beginners these senses are ignored.

Remember also, that some odors will smell different to different people. Some smells are "Universal". Dog poop and the smell of garbage are offensive to everyone. Flowers, freshly cut grass or fresh baked bread usually evoke memories. We all can picture a garden, or remember the smell of fresh cut grass (which smells different at different times of the year) and of course Mom or Grandma in the kitchen baking. Use these smells to help show us the scene or bring out an emotion of our characters.

Some smells are less universal. Cauliflower will smell differently to me than you. If the reader loves it and you hate it, the scene will be all wrong. What you want to make sound delicious might make your reader go yuck and you'll have lost the realism. Stick to the universal smells.

Pick up your favorite novel. Go through it page by page. Highlight the senses with different colors. What an amazing array of colors on the pages. No, you might not see all the colors on every page, but enough to make it colorful.

So how do we use these senses in our scenes?

Imagine your character on a beach by the ocean. Put yourself there. Close your eyes. Picture it. What do you hear? Are the seagulls squawking, children playing, waves swishing on the shore? Let's take it further. Inhale, take a deep breath. What do you smell, the fresh air, salty water, fish? How does your skin feel? Can you feel the wet spray from the waves? Can you taste the salty ocean? Wiggle your toes in the gritty sand. Is it hot, does it burn your feet? Are the waves coming on shore and flowing over your feet? Can you squish your toes in the wet sand?

How much stronger your words will be describing these feelings and tastes as well as the sights and sounds through your characters. Your story and characters will become more alive. The senses are as important to nonfiction, as they are critical to fiction. If you are writing a how to article about baking bread, the reader needs to know that they should knead the dough until it blisters for a better, lighter loaf and that it should be smooth to the touch. No the smell of the yeast is not important. Some things are not important in nonfiction, but if you are writing a nostalgic piece about the memory of Mom or Grandma baking in the kitchen, add those senses. They're an integral part of the article.

Start today, right now - observe these senses in everyday life. Pay particular attention to the feel, smell, and taste. Sometimes you can taste something just from the odor. Have you ever experienced a particularly bad odor? It smelled so bad you could almost taste it.

Remember these senses. Concentrate on the feel of the smoothness of a baby's skin or the texture of your sheets, vegetables, everything you touch. Make a mental note of these feelings. Use them in your stories. Make your characters real to the reader and enjoy the senses that we take so for granted.

One thing to remember, avoid using he/she saw, heard, felt, etc. Instead of John heard footsteps behind him. The sound of footsteps echoed behind him. Or instead of he saw someone running toward him. Someone ran toward him. John swerved to get out of the way, but not in time. He slammed into him, knocking him off his feet. Instead of he felt the touch of her hand, describe it. Lisa's soft hand slid along his arm, tender, gentle. It reminded him of another time, another place. Of Jennifer. He pulled away. He couldn't do this now. It was too soon. Her lavender perfume filled his nostrils. He hated lavender.

Practice Assignment: Rewrite the story below adding some of the senses and using the elements from Lesson 2.

The Unexpected Visitor

"Auntie Jane's here!" Alex and Amber yelled excitedly from the doorway.

Susan crawled out from under the Christmas tree, brushed herself off and turned to greet her aunt. Great! Just what she didn't need today, she thought.

"Aunt Jane, what a surprise." Susan kissed her aunt and endured her ample bosomed bear hug.

"We're just putting up the tree." Susan looked at the cluttered room and tried to explain the mess. Amber, Susan's oldest daughter, took Aunt Jane's coat while Susan moved a pile of boxes. Why had she come without calling? Susan wondered. Aunt Jane never visited this early in the season, something must be wrong.

"Your tree looks lovely, Susan." Aunt Jane plopped down on the couch. "And don't worry. I know my visit's unexpected."

Susan served coffee and pastries- relieved that at least she had them prepared. "So, Aunt Jane, what's wrong?"

"Everything's fine, dear." Aunt Jane patted the seat next to her and Alex sat down.

Susan watched Aunt Jane talk and laugh with Amber and Alex. Aunt Jane looks tired. "You are staying for dinner." She knew Aunt Jane expected to, but she asked anyway. Susan hoped she'd reveal the reason for this surprise visit at dinner.

"Of course, dear." Aunt Jane leaned back and closed her eyes.

Susan went to make dinner.

"Mama, what are we going to give Auntie Jane?" Amber asked curiously, while she helped Susan peel potatoes

"Oh no, I forgot about her gift. Do you have any ideas?"

"How come we make a big deal about her gift anyway?" Amber asked.

"Well, the tradition started years ago. Aunt Jane always brought me and my sister unique gifts. One year, she asked what we had for her. So Aunt Mary and I made her a beaded necklace." How much fun that had been. "But Aunt Jane acted like the gaudy beads were beautiful. She wore it for years every time she visited us. After that we made sure Grandma took us to the store to buy her something special. I can't believe I forgot this year."

"I'm moving to Florida for the winter." Aunt Jane made the startling announcement after dinner. She paused, looked at everyone, and smiled. "I've thought about it for a long time. These old bones can't handle much more of this cold. It's time for a warmer climate."

Alex jumped up from the table and ran from the room. She returned moments later and handed Aunt Jane a small gold box topped with a red bow. "I don't want you to forget us. Merry Christmas, Auntie Jane," Alex said happily.

Aunt Jane opened the box and took out a handmade ornament embossed with a family photograph. "Oh Alex, it's beautiful." A tear escaped her eye. "I could never forget you. And don't worry; I'll be back this summer. I promise"

Alex had found the perfect gift. Susan could tell that it held a special meaning to Aunt Jane. The unexpected visit turned out okay after all.

Extra Practice:
Describe a setting using only what you can see (visuals)
Rewrite the story adding sound
Rewrite it again adding smell
Now rewrite it adding taste
Last rewrite it incorporating touch

Do you see the difference between the first and last setting. Now of course you won't use all the senses in your settings, but you may use two or three. Try using ones other than sight and sound.

Lesson 4 –Putting it All Together

So what's the difference between show and tell? When we orally tell a story, we use our actions and different tone of voice to make our story scary, humorous, or to get our point across. When we tell the story complete with description of rooms, characters, and setting we're showing the story. Yes, it's still telling the story, but in a more powerful way.

However, when we write we don't have our tone of voice to let the reader know our character is happy or sad. In writing we can tell the story and say Uncle Joe is angry, sad, or hurt. But then you, the author, are telling the story. Authors need to show the story? We need to show the characters through actions, dialogue and thoughts, not just description? And we need to do it through our characters eyes, not the author's voice.

We already know anyone can tell a story – but it takes work to show one. It's always easier to tell than show. But with practice, as with everything in writing, it will eventually become second nature.

What do I mean by show, not tell? As we discovered in lesson one, some people think by adding adverbs, the dreaded "LY" words to the story, that it shows, but we now know that's not true.

Showing is keeping the authors voice out of the story. Any time the author's voice intrudes; it distracts from the story and sets the reader apart. We want the reader involved. We want them to feel, smell, hear, taste and see our story. So how do we do that? How do we avoid telling the story from the author's point of view?

For starters, let's talk about verbs, one of the critical parts of show. Avoiding verbs like is and was, the "to be" verbs, makes for a stronger story. The "to be" verbs show nothing. The more active a verb the better -for instance- He was going to the store. He went to the store. – He walked to the store – He hurried to the store. The first - was going - shows absolutely nothing. While walked is better than went, hurried shows us more. We can still make that a stronger sentence – He hurried to the store, head down, concentrating. Okay now we get a picture of him, but- it's still tell. How then do we make this a strong show statement? By getting into his head?

First let's give him a name. Larry will work. Larry hurried to the store. Darn always the last minute. What did she think he was? Linda never planned anything ahead of time? It's not like he had all the time in the world to run around picking up things she forgot.

See the difference? Now we can picture the character? By adding thoughts into Larry's head we know he's upset with someone - someone who can't remember to do things for herself, and he's impatient. We can tell that by the tone of his thoughts, he's feeling put upon. Thoughts are an important element to our characters. Yes, we still told that he hurried, but because we added the other the reader doesn't notice it.

We can show much with thoughts. We can show what another character looks like or acts like through our character's thoughts. Also notice I didn't use the words I or me in his thoughts. (Ex: I can't believe she didn't plan ahead. Instead, I did what they call paraphrasing and used third person. We still know Larry is thinking. By using I or me too often it begins to sound clunky, unnatural. You can use them occasionally but don't do it often or in long paragraphs, and you usually have to use the words he/she thought after them. That interferes.

Sometimes with just one word, we can show anger, sympathy, or even passion. Take the word cried, change it to sobbed or whimpered and we change the whole tone of the scene. Sobbed shows more emotion. We could say, 'she sat crying on the floor', but that only tells us she is crying. If we say she sank to the floor and sobbed - it takes more words, but we feel the emotion. It's a more powerful scene.

Look at the following example: Rose was angry. She stood with her hand on the knob when the door bell rang. She opened the door and looked into the steel gray eyes of an older man accompanied by a young girl. Rose was surprised. She stared at the man.

Compare this to - Rose grabbed the doorknob. She'd show them. She'd just go over there and let their parents know that they threw snowballs at her house. Little monsters, why didn't they leave her alone, go play in their own yards? The doorbell rang. Rose yanked the door open and confronted the steel gray eyes of an older man accompanied by the young girl. "I, it's..." Rose, seldom at a loss for words, stared at him.

In example #1 - I tell you she is angry, that she opened the door, and sees the man and that she is surprised. In example #2, I show her anger through her thoughts. She's mad at the neighborhood kids and when the bell rings she doesn't just open the door she yanks it open. Her stuttering shows her frustration. By using dialogue along with action, I let the reader figure out she's surprised. Our readers are intelligent people – they will figure it out.

Action tags are useful in showing. As I explained earlier, everyone uses body language to convey his or her emotions. We don't want to use, or should I say overuse, the words he said/she said. And we don't want to use adverbs to explain our emotions.

In the above example I could have said 'she said' or 'she stuttered' after she opened the door, but it's obvious she was stuttering so why repeat it. It's also obvious she's speaking, so why say she said? By using the action tag she stared at him, along with the statement that Rose was seldom at a loss for words shows us a little more about the kind of person Rose is.

I show a normally confident woman. And clearly the man has her flustered.

What are some of the ways you show surprise? Raised eyebrows, open mouth? Depending on personality - everyone expresses emotions differently. Some people's eyes fill with tears at just the thought of sadness, while others may out and out cry and still others may just frown or furrow their brow. Describe a scene in such a way that we show our readers emotion and bring them into the story. These emotions create our character. They show us something about their personality.

Let's look at another example. – Something hit the house. Rose got up from her chair and went to the door. She saw the kids run next door and wondered why they were bothering her.

Compare this to - A thumping noise against the house interrupted Rose's thoughts. "What in the world?" She jumped from her chair and hurried to the door. Four little pairs of legs raced around the bushes into the next yard. "Little monsters," she mumbled. "Go throw snowballs at your own house." Shaking her head, she slammed the door. "What's wrong with kids now days?"

See the difference? In the first example I tell you something hit the house, Rose got up and went to the door. You don't see anything in how she felt, or how she moved. In the second example, I show her hearing the noise and jumping up from the chair. Clearly she was in a hurry and angry. The reader experiences Rose's anger in the second example. Rose shows us, not the author's voice.

Learn to show the emotions to your reader through your character, using dialogue, action verbs, thoughts and description.

Now let's talk about adverbs again. As I stated in lesson one, an important rule is to avoid adverbs. Many new writes make the mistake of adding adverbs to the verb repeating what the verb shows us. 'She rushed hurriedly through the store.' instead of' She rushed through the store. Rushed shows us she was in a hurry, you don't need to repeat it with the word hurriedly. A strong verb will show better than an adverb. Adverbs generally tell-not show. It's important to show the story. Readers want to see the characters, relate to them, feel what they feel and we can't do that by adding adverbs. Adverbs weaken the story. They are the author's voice intruding into our relationship with our characters. There are times to use adverbs. She shook her head woodenly. If we just say she shook her head, we don't see how she shook it and since there really isn't a verb to describe woodenly it's okay to use it. It shows us how she shook it. Weigh the adverbs carefully before you use them. If it repeats the verb – DON"T use it. If you can describe it with a stronger verb – DON"T use it. If there's absolutely no other way to say it, and it's critical to the story, then use it – but use them sparingly.

When we show a story we do more to describe our characters then any adjectives. We don't need to tell the reader what the room looked like or what the character looks like, they will form their own opinions just from hearing their thoughts and seeing their actions. It is important to set the scene but do it through the characters. How then do we describe our character?

We can put them in front of a mirror - that is one over used trick to giving physical description. But we have to be careful with that. It's often another way of telling us what the character looked like. We can describe them physically in the beginning, but again the author's voice intrudes.

So how then do we get the description across to our readers?

Carolyn brushed a strand of long blond hair from her black jacket. If her hair didn't quit falling out soon, she'd be bald before she turned thirty. The doctor said nerves caused it, but she wasn't so sure. After all what did she have to be nervous about? Her upcoming wedding? Not likely, she and Stephen were ecstatic and enjoyed making plans.

Okay we know Carolyn has long blond hair and isn't yet thirty, and you, the author didn't tell us. The reader can surmise the hairstyle, but we know it's long. Our readers will all picture a different character than you picture anyway. No two readers will picture what you pictured for your character – and that's okay. As long as we make it clear in the beginning of the story the age of our character. There's nothing worse than reading about a character and two chapters later discover the young woman we thought we were reading about is really a sixty-five year old grandmother. We need to introduce this in some way early on in the story as I did with Carolyn.

Now that doesn't mean you need to tell us the age of your character, but through some action as with Carolyn's thoughts, we need to figure out an approximate age. Take Carolyn, with long blond hair and her upcoming wedding and thinking she'll be bald before she's thirty, we know she isn't a sixty-five year old grandmother. We could have made her older, many women get married after thirty but that added thought tells us she's in her twenties. We need to let the reader know something about her to indicate her age. If she were older, we could change the age she'd be bald to 50 or 60 or we could make reference to what did she have to be nervous about? Her upcoming wedding. It wasn't as if this was her first, she had experience with these things. That would show she's been married before.

But does it make a difference? Can the reader put her at the age they want, as long as they know she's not an old woman? Certainly, if it's not important to the story, however if Carolyn's age has something to do with the plot then we'll figure a way to show her age as I did in my example. Another way is to have her think about her last birthday.

It wasn't so bad turning forty, why did everyone make such a big deal out of it? It's just another year and Marie still felt young so what's the big to do? Or use any age. There are many ways to show an age without coming right out and saying

Carolyn was twenty-five, thirty or forty. Readers do like to have an idea of the character's age group.

Now, let's go back to verbs. Let's look at the word walked again. Our character can amble, race, creep, mosey, shuffle, trot or many other various forms. Each one shows a different mood. If he moseys along, we know he has all the time in the world, compared to if he raced, unless he's dawdling to avoid something, but you'd have to show that. John strolled through the park, stopping to watch a group of children on the swings. You'd think he had all the time in the world, when in fact, he was late. The later the better as far as he was concerned. Sylvia wanted to discuss the terms of their divorce. Divorce! He didn't want the separation, what the heck made her think he'd be thrilled about a divorce?

If he shuffles we may see an old man or maybe someone ill. The different verbs add many characteristic and can even add emotion or tension to a story.

Not only do verbs show action, they set the emotional tone. So next time you're tempted to write 'Susan didn't like the idea she was going to be late- change it to 'Susan hated the idea of being late. It shows us Susan is usually on time - an important characteristic. And don't forget the thoughts, these show us the real character and set a tone and mood for them.

Last but, certainly, not least, are the senses. We learned how important sight (visuals), hearing (sounds), taste (flavors), and touch (texture) are to our story. It brings our characters and settings alive - Makes our story more believable. Certainly, in short stories, there will be limited senses but in everyday life, we deal with all of our sense. Leave these out and our story will lack credibility. Our readers may not know why, but they'll know something is missing. The longer the story or novel, the more we need to touch on all of the senses.

Showing is visual, telling is just that- telling. By adding descriptive action to the story we show what's happening, through the characters eyes. Telling is the process the author, himself, telling the story. If you can show the descriptive action your readers will visualize the story, therefore putting themselves in the story (living it) and removing you from the narration. All writing is a form of telling in so far as the author controls it.

When I sit down to write a story, I want to show my readers what my characters are feeling, seeing, hearing, tasting, and yes, even smelling. I want to pull my readers in, make them want to continue reading. I want them to picture my characters or better yet put themselves in my characters place. I'm sure you've read books that held you spellbound. The author showed those stories. We didn't want to put the book down until we finished. That's what we want to accomplish. We want the reader to become involved in the story setting and the character. By showing our readers the characters through thoughts and actions, we're showing something of our character that we didn't tell.

Below is a list of words to avoid. They can often be replaced with stronger words or just omitted altogether.

LY words (adverbs) of course, but also avoid these words:
Of, this, was, very, about, and, were, but, by, felt, like, saw, watched, heard, thought, that, could, would, noticed

Practice Assignment:
Write your own story or partial story of approximately 500 words using what you've learned from all four of the lessons.

You may use any of the stories I used for examples or make up your own.

Extra practice: Practice writing paragraphs with adverbs, then go back and edit them out using the examples I gave in Assignment 1.

Practice writing paragraphs with he said/she said. Then go back and add the 3 elements from Assignment 2

Practice writing paragraphs using as many of the senses as you can. Over do it, then go back and take some away.

Remember the best way to learn good writing is to WRITE, WRITE, and WRITE!!! As you've probably heard many times about many things – Practice makes perfect. And have fun with it.

Thank you for taking my course, I hope I helped you. If you ever have questions in the future email me I'll be glad to answer them.

Part 2 – Self Editing

Lesson 1 – More About Showing, not telling and editing

Editing is, by far, the most difficult part of writing. Okay, one of the most difficult. Editing is where we have to cut precious words, sentences, or maybe even whole paragraphs. How do we even go about editing? Most of us know to look for punctuation, that's the easy part. After all we've all learned about commas, periods, question marks and exclamation marks in school, didn't we?
Even if we forgot most of what we learned, there are books to help refresh us. But what about the other parts of editing. More importantly, what are the other parts?
Did we show, instead of tell? Have we created our characters and shown them without the author's voice interfering? Have we created enough description?
How about describing our surroundings and other scenes. Have we added the five elements necessary to our story? Are our POV's consistent or have we head hopped all over the place? Have we used the proper dialogue? Added thoughts and action tags? Avoided adverbs or other unnecessary words? Proper editing takes almost as much time as writing.

One of the most important things in editing is showing and eliminating the "to be" verbs – is, was, were, are, etc. These verbs show nothing. Use strong action verbs.

Often times, the 'to be' verb are used with an 'ing' word. You can always – always_– drop the 'to be' verb and change the verb to past tense. Example – was walking – walked, is singing - sang, were running – ran, are laughing – laughed.

What exactly does all of this mean? Simple – Showing keeps up the pace of the story. Adds action, emotion, thoughts. Let's take an example:

Telling: Wendy was walking through the airport. Suddenly, someone bumped her. She fell. She dropped her carry-on bag. Someone fell on top of her. She couldn't breathe.

OR

Showing: "Ugh!" What the heck? Wendy's feet slid out from under her. Splat, she landed flat on her back. Her carry-on skidded across the floor. Someone fell on top of her and pinned to the floor, the breath knocked out of her.

Which one sounds better to you? Do we learn a bit about Wendy from the 2nd description? Obviously, she was in a hurry, and now she's angry. But we also get a much better picture of the scene through the second example.

Also avoid the need to explain. In the above example, I could have said she fell, and she was angry. I'd rather show that to my readers. Let them figure it out. Readers are smart people; we don't have to explain everything to them.

There are, of course, other ways to show anger. Slamming a fist on the table, hitting a steering wheel, kicking a piece of dirt. Think about ways you show anger, besides the obvious of yelling. Our actions often show anger. In the above, the - what the heck, was Wendy's thoughts. Our character's thoughts show the reader many things.

Avoid phrases like tried to, began, started, and use the past tense verb. These phrases weaken what you're saying. Past tense verbs are more active.

EX: The aroma of sauce seemed to fill the room.
Better: The aroma of sauce filled the room. Or - The aroma of sauce reached Josh's nostrils. Gosh he was hungrier than he thought. Shows a bit more.

EX: George tried to start the report again.
Better: George started the report for the third time. If he could just get her out of his mind, he might just finish it tonight. – Shows what's distracting him.
on each page. Writers often forget touch and taste. As I stated earlier, if you leave them out, the reader

will notice something is missing. Taste and touch are just as important as sight, sound, and smell.

Practice Assignment:

Rewrite the paragraph below using what you learned in this lesson.

Meg sat down. She was so tired. She wished the day was over. She looked at her watch. It was only 9:00. She still had three hours to go.
Sarah came over and sat down next to Meg. "What's the matter with you?" she asked quietly.
"I'm so tired. I didn't sleep well last night and I got up too early this morning. Bob called and we had a fight. He isn't coming to the party with me. I'm so upset with him." Meg replied.
"Oh that's too bad. Why isn't he coming with you?" Sarah asked.
Meg stood up. She was so angry she didn't want to talk anymore. "I have to go. I still need to eat."
Meg went into the small restaurant. Something smelled good. It smelled like spaghetti sauce. Meg didn't realize how hungry she was until now. She started to walk to her table and the waiter stopped her.

"I'm sorry, miss. You have to wait for the hostess to seat you," the waiter said.
"Oh, I'm sorry. I didn't see anyone," Meg replied and went to the foyer.

Lesson 2- More About Creating and describing your characters, places and things.

Avoid describing your characters from the author's, point of view.

Example – through the author's voice – He was sexy. His jeans hugged his hips and he was very muscular. He walked with a long stride. He looked very sure of himself.
This interferes with our characters.
Instead, describe him through another character or even from themselves. You can do it through dialogue or thoughts.

Example – dialogue: "Darn, he's sexy. Look at the way those jeans hug his butt. And those muscles. Honestly, Lucy, have you ever seen such a hunk before?" Susan stared at him. "And that long, easy stride reeks confidence. I'd sure like to know him better."

Example – thoughts- Susan couldn't help but stare at him. Darn he had to be the sexiest man she'd ever seen. The way those jeans hugged his hips and those muscles. Lord, he sure was a hunk. His long easy stride reeked confidence. Definitely sure of himself.

The kind of man, she'd like to get to know. Now how to go about getting an introduction.

The above examples describe the man and show something about him. Besides being sexy, muscular, and a hunk, he shows confidence. In both examples we learn Susan wants to meet him. This helps move our story along.

It's not necessary to give extra information if it's not important to the story. At this point it's not necessary to know he has blue eyes and blond hair. Or that his nose looks broken and his jaw juts out when he's thinking. We can learn that later. For the above scene this was just the right amount of information. Later, when Susan introduces herself, or gets an introduction through a third party, we can learn the color of his eyes, his height, hair color or any other information that's pertinent at that moment. The reader doesn't need to know everything about the character at once.

How do we describe a character from his/her own POV? Some authors chose to use mirrors, but that's a bit overdone. There are other ways to impart information about our character from themselves.

Example 1 – Karen straightened to her full height and swished her blond hair out of her face.. Wasn't so bad being tall. Right now, she liked it. It gave her a feeling of confidence. Great feeling for a twenty year old. Now to meet that handsome hunk.

Example 2 – Turning forty wasn't so bad. Shelly didn't feel any different. Why did people make such a big deal about it? Her hair hadn't gone bald or turned gray overnight. In fact she still had a full head of auburn hair. Age was just mind over matter. If you didn't mind, it didn't matter.

In each of the examples above I show their age, color of hair. In the first one I show she's tall also. Okay I don't say how tall, but the reader can decide that for themselves. It's not necessary to explain everything.   I also show that they're confident women.

How about describing your surroundings? That depends on your character and the circumstances. Some people notice things others don't. If you love flowers, you'll notice the first bloom in the spring. If you're not a flower person, you won't notice. Know your character and keep this consistent.   On the other hand, even a person who loves flowers isn't going to notice them if someone has a gun aimed at their face.

Don't let the author's voice interfere – John liked flowers. He looked at the tulips. They were such vivid colors. Lily loved tulips too. He would stop at the florist and send her a bouquet. That's telling.

Example: John strolled down the street. Ah, Spring. He loved this time of year, loved the crisp, fresh air.

Nothing like the smell of spring. Already the daffodils and tulips bloomed and buds formed on the trees. And the tulips, such vivid colors. Out of all the flowers, tulips were his favorites. He made a mental note to stop at the florist to send a bouquet to Lily. She loved tulips almost as much as he did.

From the above example we learn John isn't in a hurry. He strolled – which means he took his time. He loves spring and flowers. We also learn a bit about Lily. She loves tulips too. Makes us curious about Lily. We wonder who she is. We want to read more.

The same applies to describing a room – If a character isn't into antiques, they wouldn't notice the family heirloom standing in the corner. If they weren't much into furniture, or decoration, they probably wouldn't notice much at all. That's why it's important to know your characters likes and dislikes. Using the character worksheets for each character helps keep them straight, also. It's important to know everything about our character or our descriptions will sound false. I happen to love antiques so at least one of my characters will also.

Ex: Samantha headed for the curved stairway. Never had she seen anything like it. The way it floated to the second floor with no signs that anything held it up. The beauty of the walnut treads set off the bright white baluster and handrail. Definitely the focal point of the Victorian room.

Most people probably wouldn't notice the stairway, nor the colors. But if your character is into antiques or Victorian homes, or a designer, these things would stand out to him/her.

Using thoughts – As I said earlier, thoughts are as important as action and dialogue in showing. The third leg of the tripod so to speak. We show a lot of information from the character's thoughts. How many times have you thought – oh right – when someone was speaking to you? I have, especially if I don't agree. I might not speak these thoughts to avoid an argument or to avoid hurting someone's feelings. The same should be true for our characters. Maybe the other person is thinking about how the other character looks or they'd like to run their fingers through their hair or push a stray strand of hair away from their face. When someone is speaking, our mind is constantly working, noticing things, and forming ideas of what to reply. We can show a lot of what someone looks like through thoughts. Instead of saying he wore pants that were too short and a shirt that was too tight, do it through your hero or heroine. Mike almost burst out laughing. Who gave George the clothes? His skinny, bony legs stuck out of his too short pants and the buttons on his shirt were ready to pop. Couldn't he have found someone his own size to borrow clothes from?

Avoid using "I in thoughts. The use of "I" makes it sound clunky. It's better to paraphrase with she/he. The reader still knows the character is thinking.

Again, I'm going to reiterate to avoid the "to be" verbs – is, was, are etc. They show nothing. Yes, there are times we can't avoid using them, especially in dialogue. As with adverbs, use them sparingly.

Assignment: Using what you learned rewrite the paragraph below.

"Nine, one, one emergency," the operator said. "What is your emergency?"

"Help please! Someone followed me home." Leslie went from her car to the house. Struggling to get her key in the lock, she said her name and address to the operator. She heard footsteps pounding in her ears.

"Closer. He's getting closer. The door won't..." The lock turned. The door opened.

"I'm in..." Pushing the door closed behind her, she saw his hand curl around the edge. "Oh my God, Oh my God, he's in the house," she said.

She went up the three steps to the kitchen. Seeing Rob's baseball bat in the corner, she dropped her phone, grabbed the bat, turned, and swung it with all her might. The man fell to the landing at the bottom of the steps. A pool of blood gushed from his head.

"I hit him... Oh Lord, I think I killed him," she said. Her knees buckled, she collapsed on the steps. Tears streamed down her cheeks.

"The police are on their way, calm down." The operator said. "Ma'am can you hear me?"

Leslie picked up her phone. "He's not moving, I think he's dead." I know I killed him. He's not moving. Oh God, I killed a man.

Sirens sounded in the distance. Eyes blurred, she wrapped her arms around her knees, leaned forward, and vomited.

"Ma'am, Ma'am, excuse me, Ma'am are you all right?" Someone said and touched her shoulder.

She screamed - pulled back.

"It's okay, Ma'am, I'm a police officer. We're going to get you out of here, come on." He helped her to her feet and led her through the house and out the front door, away from the sight of the hideous man with his bloody smashed head.

Leslie shivered and hugged herself tighter, and leaned against the officer wearily. He led her around the house, into the backyard and pulled out a chair on the patio. Someone brought her water.

She took a sip to rid her mouth of the bitter bile taste. Police officers swarmed the yard and the house. Police cars, sirens blaring, still arrived on the scene. An ambulance arrived. Two men pulled a gurney piled with equipment. They went into the house.

"He's dead. I know he's dead." She said to no one specific. She rocked on the chair. She crossed her arms in front of her. Why was she so cold, she wondered?

This is a nightmare, she thought. It can't be happening. She watched everything as if in slow motion. Her body went from cold to hot, back to cold. She closed her eyes. When I open them, this will all be like a bad dream.

She opened her eyes and looked up to see Rob. He stopped while they brought out the body, then he came toward her. He held out his arms. Leslie stood up and fell into them.

Lesson 3 – Keeping your POV consistent

Years ago stories were written from one point of view. Since then, especially in romance, more than one POV is often used. First, let's talk a bit about POV. There are several different ways to write - First person POV or third person POV. Some writers write omniscient POV.

POV helps the writer paint a picture of the setting around the character and also helps the reader get to know the characters. It helps the reader care, or dislike, the characters. The more an author delves into a character, the more the reader becomes involved.

It's important for the author to have the reader become absorbed in the character, especially in the beginning of the book. Avoid passive POV – Everything the character hears, smells, sees, touches and thinks is shown through POV. Even the reactions and feelings of other characters can be relayed through the POV character. If done correctly you can eliminate the use of "he thought" or "he watched" it's redundant. Leave it out. Looks for telling words like the ones below and eliminate them: Saw, Heard, Felt, Watched, Thought, Knew

They tell, not show.

EX: Not this – Joe saw the waiter carry a plate of spaghetti and meatballs past him. That looked good.

This – The waiter carried a plate of spaghetti and meatballs past Joe. They smelled and looked delicious, that's what he'd order.

Not this: She heard the bells ring.
This – The bells rang. (We know she heard it if it rang)

Back to POV have to decide which POV voice you want to use.

First person is the "I" voice. Everything is spoken through the first person. Everything is seen through the first person. The minute I came into the room something didn't feel right. It took me a moment to realize what it was. Mary's jewelry was on the dresser. Mary never left her jewelry sitting out that way.

This point of view has its advantages as well as draw backs. You can give the reader a sense of detail. In fact the reader is in the character's head, so to speak. One of the disadvantages is you always have to be on the scene. The reader can't see anything except through your eyes. The reader isn't allowed to know what the other characters are thinking except through your point of view. It's limiting.

Omniscient point of view is the complete opposite of first person. It's not used a lot and reasonably so.

Scenes written in this point of view show us the inside of everyone's head. We don't become intimate with any of the characters. Obviously, this is not a good point of view. Some writers do it and get away with it. Some even do it well. For a new writer, I'd avoid this POV.

The easiest – in my opinion- is third person point of view. The third person provides a combination of viewpoint and familiarity. With third person point of view you can change between characters, giving their points of view. Just be careful not to give everyone's point of view. Limit it to two, not more than three main characters. Also, keep to one character's points of view per scene.

How to keep point of view consistent – With first person, obviously, it's easy. There's only one point of view. You can't show anyone else's.

I won't discuss omniscient since that should be avoided.

In third person point of view, you need to limit one point of view per scene. I know some well-known authors use more than one. But that's called head-hopping and can confuse the reader. Some writers do it smoothly and get away with it. It's best, however to use only one point of view per scene.

Establish the point of view early in the scene - In the first sentence if possible.

As I said earlier make sure you know your character. A rough, tough guy wouldn't sound like a mamby pamby. Picture a rough tough character describing a flower using words like ravishing, delicate. More than likely, he wouldn't even notice a flower, but if he did (I suppose some rough guys liked flowers) he'd use different words. I'm sure even rough guys have a sensitive side. In fact, it would be a surprise for readers. . But let's face it we sure don't picture them that way. Also a man from the Victorian era wouldn't sound like a man from the late 20th century, let alone the way we speak today.

Remember also, to make your characters sound different. If all the characters sound the same, it's boring. Each character should have different emotions - Should react differently to the same circumstances. People are different. Our characters need to be also.

By sticking to one character's point of view per scene, we build suspense. Our character can only surmise what the other is thinking by their facial expressions and actions.
Example: Liz's father's expression changed from one of disgust to downright rage. The way his veins popped out on his forehead scared her. She swore one of these days they were going to burst. That wasn't good. She was in for it big time and there wasn't a darn thing she could do to stop it. She'd have to stand here and listen to another of his lectures.

We know from Liz's point of view that her father is angry. Worse than angry, he's in a rage and she's in for a long lecture. Now I could have used her father's point of view and showed exactly what he was thinking but this way is so much better. It gives us a much better picture of him form Liz's viewpoint. In the next scene we can delve into her father's head, if we wish. But Liz is the main character, the heroine. Her father plays a secondary role.

Okay, we know how to establish one point of view. We know how to show how the other person is acting through that point of view. How do we change points of view? It's simple. We end that scene and move to another. We insert a line space or **** to show the reader the scene is changing or we change chapters. That way our readers aren't taken by surprise. Now don't get the idea you can do this with every paragraph or person's dialogue. Stick to the same person's point of view throughout the scene. Let's say we're in the heroine's point of view. Everything, including the actions of the hero, is described from what she's seeing.

Example:

After dinner, Michele escaped to the restroom. She needed to recuperate from Brad's surprising devotion. He had played his part well, too well. She brushed her fingers across her lips where moments before Brad had planted his most passionate kiss yet. He had ignited a charge in her that began slow and increased with the pressure of his lips. By the time he pulled away, her body wanted to explode. Her head swirled, and their guests shouted for more. She had no idea Brad kissed that good. This wasn't part of the deal.

She wanted a moment to herself, needed to regroup. But Ruby, Brad's assistant and ex-girlfriend came in right behind her.

"Well, well, the happy bride." Sarcasm and bitterness dripped from Ruby's voice.

Michele took a step backwards. She didn't like Ruby, never had. What Brad saw in the woman, she'd never know. But right now she didn't like the confrontational attitude of his assistant and former girlfriend. She turned away, ignoring Ruby.

Ruby moved closer and swished her long, straw-colored hair. "Just remember, sweetie, you might sleep on his satin sheets, but I'll always have his heart." She paused and glared at Michele.

"Remember that when he tells you he has to work late or takes a sudden business trip." Ruby pointed her finger under Michele's nose and anger flickered in her icy blue eyes. "And then picture him in bed with me." With that, she turned and strode out of the room, her thin hips swinging sexily.

Michele took a deep breath, her insides turned summersaults, her legs turned to jelly. The ugly sneer on Ruby's face rattled her. She certainly hadn't pulled any punches. Anger flared in Michele. How dare that witch follow her in here like that? And darn Brad anyhow, that relationship was supposed to be long over. He had promised that he'd be faithful. Why had he invited her to the wedding?

Mutual respect and faithfulness Brad had said. Honesty. Well this sure didn't sound like Brad meant to keep that promise, did it? Minutes that seemed like hours passed before Michele composed herself enough to return to her husband and guests. When she rounded the corner of the hall, she sought out Brad and immediately picked him out.

Him and Ruby.

Michele grimaced at the way Brad's arm rested comfortably around Ruby's shoulders and the way their heads met, in intimate conversation. Ruby threw her head back, laughed, and snuggled into Brad's chest. Their gaze locked and held. Michele backed into the alcove near the doorway. Renewed anger welled up in her. Ruby was flirting with Brad right under her nose. And Brad sure wasn't resisting. A tightening around her heart surprised her. Why should she care if Brad strayed?

Because he promised. He had agreed they wouldn't embarrass each other with indiscretions. Indiscretions, Ha! Look at them right in plain view. Michele pulled herself together, straightened to her full five foot, eight height, and took a deep breath, determined to carry their act through the remainder of the evening. She'd act as if she were madly in love with her new husband. Coughing to announce herself, she came out of the shadows. She took Brad's arm and managed to disengage him from Ruby's clutches. "We should make the rounds with our guests."

"You're right." Brad took her arm and they went back to the hall.

***

Michele's action surprised Brad. It sure didn't fit her usual behavior. He had waited for her to return from the restroom so they could make their rounds of the guests. Unfortunately, Ruby came out first and cornered him. They were in a deep discussion concerning work, which Brad would have preferred to forget for one night of his life. Suddenly Michele was at his side, taking his arm in a possessive way. The warmth of her hand felt good on his arm, and he almost laughed aloud at the way she managed to release him from Ruby's grip. Did he detect a hint of jealousy? Was there something more to his wife's feelings for him? He had tried several times to move away from Ruby, and in one swift movement, Michele accomplished it, just like that. And the glare Michele threw Ruby. He almost felt the pain of those daggers himself. Looks like his wife had a temper.

Most of the scene is set in Michele's POV. When she disengages Ruby from Brad and they return to the hall, the scene ends. We then pick up Brad's point of view. Notice the line break between the two pov's.

Practice Assignment: Rewrite the paragraph below using what you learned in the previous lessons.

She ran her fingers through her hair. She cringed. She spent one night in the jail. It made her itchy. She felt like a million bugs crawled all over her. She looked at the handful of gray hair. It was falling out. She was only sixty, why was her hair falling out? When she got out, she was going to have to see what the problem was. Right now she was worried about how to get out of jail. She wanted now was a hot shower and warm bed. She wondered where Jim Landry was.

What kind of police chief goes fishing in the middle of the week? Jessica rubbed her wrists. Officer Edwards handcuffed her. It hurt her and humiliated her. He seemed to take pleasure in making sure they were real snug too. He was a smart ass rookie cop. Didn't he know who she was?

Of course he knew, that's why he took such pleasure. He was paying her back because she reproached him in her court room when he testified in that hit and run case. He was too smart for his own good. He had a cocky attitude.

Jessica put her hand in her pocket and felt the button in her pocket. It was a clue, she knew it. She knew she shouldn't have picked it up from the crime scene, but she had it in her hand when Edwards came along. He yelled she was under arrest. She barely had enough time to drop it in her pocket when he slapped the cuffs on her.

Darn, she wished she knew what Jake had wanted. He was so secretive calling and asked her to meet him in that alley. Good lord, they were no better than thugs. He said something about police corruption and he couldn't talk to Landry about it. What in the world did that mean? Landry was the most honest cop she knew. He wouldn't cheat a store clerk out of a penny.

"Jess, what the hell's going on?" Landry said. His voice boomed through the cell. Something fishy was going on here. Jess shouldn't be in jail.

"About time you got here. How should I know what's going on? Someone killed Jake Warren, and that officer out there seems to think it was me." She was tired and cold and wanted to go home. Now if the Chief would open the cell and get her out of here.

"Hmm." Chief Landry rubbed his unshaven chin. "Well everyone in town knows you and Jake didn't see eye to eye." Jess looked like hell. Poor thing. Her hair was a mess, her clothes were dirty. Her mascara was smeared.

"You can't believe I had anything to do with his death," Jessica said. She glared at Chief Landry. "No, we didn't see eye to eye, but you can't possibly believe I killed him. Good Lord, Jim you know me better than that." Even as a joke this wasn't funny. "Come on open the door - get me out of here."

"Well, I'd like to do that, Jess, but see, you've been booked, and we have to follow procedure. You know the proper channels." He unlocked the door and motioned to her. "Come on we'll talk in my office."

Pushing the door open, Jess followed him.

Lesson 4 – Proper dialogue, tags, and thoughts

One of the most important things when writing dialogue is the tags. We talked about them earlier. We already know not to use adverbs when a stronger verb works better. They show us NOTHING, and repeat the action verb.

Also avoid the use of words like snort, laughed or grimaced as tags, we can't laugh, snort, or grimace a sentence. They brand you as an amateur. If you must use a tag to show who says something use said.

As stated earlier, readers don't notice it. It blends in. Use of words like replied, demanded, inquired, offered and asked (especially after a question mark, the question mark shows someone asked – it's repetitive). Use of these words draws attention away from the dialogue. And we never want the reader drawn away from the story. Said is almost invisible to the reader. Also remember to put he/she or the name of the person speaking first. He said, she said, Dave said. Though authors sometimes use 'said Dave' – but using said first is awkward and less professional.

Of course no one wants to read a whole page of he said/she said either. The use of action tags or thoughts eliminates this problem. If there are only two people speaking and it's clear who is saying what, eliminate a tag altogether.

Example: "Who said that, Liz?"

"Look, Bill, I'm not going and that's that.

That makes it very clear who is speaking and to whom. However, that's okay once in a while. Using a person's name in a sentence is fine occasionally, but we wouldn't want to see a whole page of it. Besides, people don't speak that way in real life why would your characters?

Another way to avoid using a page of he said/she said is to use action tags - "I can't go tonight." Bill looked away. "I really wish I could, but I promised Samantha I'd help her."

Again, we don't want a whole page of action tags either. Sometimes thoughts work well in place of dialogue tags. Bob reached out and grabbed her before she fell. "Oops, sorry." He looked down at her. Damn, she had the greenest eyes he ever saw. He pulled her to her feet and had the irresistible urge to kiss her. He'd better get control and darn quick. What was the matter with him? (notice I didn't use he thought and I paraphrased rather than using I)

Also, remember to start a new paragraph with each speaker. If you have a long paragraph of dialogue from one person, break it up with tags, either action or thoughts and sometimes start a new paragraph.

Some things to Check - Check your dialogue for emotion. Get rid of the adverbs. Look for the speaker attributions – things that are physically impossible – grimaced etc. Also get rid of verbs other than said, like replied, demanded, etc. Use said or action tags and thoughts. You can use an occasional – answered, replied just don't do it often, they take the reader out of the story.

Try getting rid of the speaker attributions completely and see if you still know who is speaking. If you can, eliminate them. Make sure to start a new paragraph with each speaker.

Use ellipsis for gaps, dashes for interruptions. Read dialogue aloud. We don't talk on and on, make sure your characters don't either. Short paragraphs add tension. Be careful not to repeat a word too closely together. More than once in a sentence or couple of sentences.

When you read your dialogue aloud, does it sound the way we speak? Make sure it's the way your characters speak. Sometimes we speak using sentence fragments. And don't forget contractions. We seldom say can not, is not etc. We shorten it to can't, isn't etc. Unless we have a very well educated, stiff, formal character seldom will our characters use perfect English. We also use slang, so should our character – if the character isn't an intellect – college professor or English major.. A construction worker probably wouldn't use the word colleague, nor would a boxer, wrestler or any rough-type hero. On the other hand, a gentlemen type character probably wouldn't say gonna or use slang. Know your characters.

Practice Assignment:

Change the adverbs in the story below to strong verbs and change the whole tone of the story, showing instead of telling. You can expand on it if you wish and use everything you've learned so far.. You can change the sentence structure if you want, but stick to the same story elements.

John walked hurriedly. He thought about his argument with Sarah. Sarah sure had yelled loud enough. He had made her so mad. He never heard her yell so loudly.

He remembered her words. "How could you do something so stupid, John?" she yelled loudly. Then she threw the ring angrily across the room.

He felt in his pocket and took out the ring. He couldn't believe she threw it across the room. She was mad because he put it on the charge account.

"I don't need a ring that big," she cried angrily. Slowly she had turned and left him standing alone.

He was on his way to take the ring back. He went into the store cautiously. He didn't know how he was going to explain this.

"Excuse me," he said hesitantly.
The man behind the counter looked up. "Can I help you?"

"I, uh, yes, I bought this ring yesterday and um." John coughed softly to cover up his embarrassment.

"I understand," the man behind the counter said sympathetically. "She doesn't want to get married right now. That's okay we'll take the ring back."

John gave the man his receipt. He sighed loudly, relieved. At least he wouldn't have a big bill now. He looked at cheaper rings but decided to bring Sarah in to pick out one she'd like. Hopefully she would agree.

He left the store and walked quickly home. He wanted to find Sarah and tell her the good news. Now he didn't have the big bill and she'd have to forgive him.

"Sarah, guess what. I took the ring back and they took it off my bill." John said laughingly.

" That's great, John. I feel much better now. We can't start our marriage off with a big bill like that," Sarah said happily.

John placed his hand on her back gently and kissed her cheek. "Would you come with me to pick out your ring?" he asked slowly.

Sarah looked at him lovingly. "Sure, John, but you know it's not going to be as big as the one you picked out. I want you to buy something you can afford." She rubbed her finger along his cheek tenderly. "I didn't mean to get so angry at you. I just knew you over extended yourself and I didn't want our marriage to be bogged down with that kind of expense. We have to save every penny for our wedding.

John let out a big sigh of relief. He knew Sarah was right. He knew she'd make a good wife. She watched her money frugally and wouldn't spend wastefully. "I love you, Sarah McCoy." He said affectionately.

"I love you, too, John Stewart." Sarah smiled dreamily.

Lesson 5 – Common Mistakes

One of the first and most important things to do before editing is to let your manuscript sit for at least a week. I usually let mine sit longer – a month to 3 months. You need to get away from it for a while, forget about it. When you come back to it, it'll be with fresh eyes. If you look at it too soon, the story is too fresh in your mind, you'll read what you meant to write, not what you actually wrote.

Some people print the manuscript out to proofread it on paper rather than a computer. Whichever works for you is fine. If you use a paper copy, mark it up and come back with to the computer. Use the search engine to look for words you overuse – such as 'that'. Most times it can be eliminated. We'll talk more about that later.

One of the things to look for is contractions - It's is the contraction for it is – its is possessive. Who's is the contraction for who is – whose is possessive. You're for you are – your is possessive – they're is they are – their is possessive, there is a place.

Possessive pronouns never use apostrophes. Let's is a contraction for let us. Plurals don't use apostrophes, just an s. An apostrophe s makes the word possessive. The boys are home. The boy's dog is lost.

Overuse of the word 'that'. As I said earlier, most times it can be deleted. I know we use it a lot when we're speaking, but unless it's in dialogue – get rid of it when you can. Read the sentence without it. If it makes sense you don't need it. And then is another overuse. Often and can be used alone. Sometimes it's best to make two sentences.

Watch verb tenses – keep them consistent especially in compound sentences. If you use a past tense in the first part, use a past tense in the second.

Example: He walked down the street and falls on the curb is not consistent. Both verbs need to be past tense or both verbs need to be present. He walked down the street and fell on the curb. Or he walks down the street and falls on the curb. I, personally, have a problem with present tense. It doesn't seem to bother other readers, but my thought is – once something happens it immediately becomes the past.

The sentence I just wrote is done – it's finished. Therefore it's not – the sentence I write is done. It just doesn't make sense to me to write a whole book – three hundred and some pages – of present tense. But, like I said – that's my view point. Everyone doesn't agree because there's thousands of a book, good ones, I might add – written in present tense. For some reason, I've yet to figure out why writers seem to do it more when writing in first person. I'm not sure why they think it makes more sense to write I walk to the store instead of I walked to the store. Whichever you chose, keep it consistent. But I digress.

Another common mistake is I and me or he and him, etc. I find a simple way to decide which is correct is simply to eliminate the he/she and before I. If it makes sense use I, if not it's me. Example. He and I went to the store. Eliminate 'He' and the sentence reads I went to the store. It makes sense - I is correct. She gave the money to him and me. Eliminate 'him' and the sentence and the sentence reads, she gave the money to me, which makes sense, so me is correct. I and me is being misused more and more in every day language, even on TV. It drives me crazy.

The he and him can be replaced with names and it still works. I won't go into the grammar explanation of the words being a subject or an object because this is how I was taught to figure out their use and to me it's easier.

Vary the length of your sentences. Sometimes shorter sentences are better than long ones. Its fine to use a compound sentence occasionally, but if you use too many, or if your sentence is so long that if you were reading it aloud, you'd run out of breath, much like this sentence. Vary the length of your sentences for pacing. But don't get carried away with too many long and compound sentences. Short, choppy sentences add tension. So sometimes it's good to have a string of short sentences, depending on the scene.

Too means also, two is a number, to is a preposition. Lie is when you lie down on a bed, lay is what you do, like lay an object down. The past tense of lie is lay. That starts to get complicated. I wouldn't correct it in dialogue, since most people commonly make the mistake and we want our dialogue realistic.

Be careful with 'ing' words. If you begin a sentence with an 'ing' word, the action has to be physically possible to carry through to the end of the sentence.

Example – Getting into the car, I turned the ignition. Impossible. You have to be in the car to turn on the ignition, you can't do it while you're getting into it.

Sighing, I got into the car and turned the ignition. That is correct because your sigh can carry through while you get into the car and turn the ignition. Of course that would be a long sigh.

Remember to avoid 'ly' words. Use strong verbs instead. Avoid beginning a sentence with the word 'there' it becomes too wordy. Example – There was a dark cloud moving across the sky. For starters – was is a 'to be' verb and we know to avoid them. The sentence reads much better this way – A dark cloud moved across the sky. Shorter more descriptive and stronger.

Too much of anything is wasteful. There's an old saying – less is more. That applies to writing also. Avoid too many italicized words, exclamation points, metaphors, and profanity. They're much more effective if used sparingly to get your point across.

Make sure there's only one space between words and sentences, one period at the end of your sentence. Watch for misspelled words – word catches a lot of them, but often misspelled words are actual words. Example – see, sea, and seen, word won't catch the misspelling since all three are words.

Punctuation- One of the mistakes new writers make most often is the punctuation within quotes. A comma only goes before the quotation marks if you follow it by said or some variation of said, replied, asked, answered, etc. If an action tag or thought follows the quotes, use a period.

Ex: "John, please come here," Lisa said.
"John, please come here." Lisa stood near the window.

Punctuation always belongs inside quotation marks. He moved from "North," to "South," and back to "North" again.

Commas generally go before or after 'ing' words or phrases. Going along for the ride, I tried to keep up with the pace.. Kelly fixed dinner, making sure everything was cooked just so.

Commas also go after phrases often beginning with When or As – Example – When the door banged, Susan jumped. As the judge came in, the crowd quieted.

Commas are used in compound sentences joined by and/but where the period would go if they were two sentences. Jamie giggled, and I turned to see what was so funny.

Avoid ending a sentence with a prepositional phrase that is usually implied– to him, for her, at him. Example: I gave the book to him. Instead – I gave him the book.

Lesson 6 – Formatting our Manuscripts.

As I stated earlier, editing is one of the most difficult parts of writing. We slave over our work for days, weeks, months, even years, and now we're asked to cut out precious words, sentences, paragraphs, or even whole scenes. Not to mention it takes time. Lots of time.

I'll give you some hints on how to make it easier. You may already know how to do it. First, I want to talk about proper formatting for the manuscript. As an editor, it's amazing the different formats I received.

First and foremost. Set the margins. Click on Page Layout. Below that click on Page Setup. On the margin tab, set top, bottom, left and right to 1".

Now slide over and click on paragraph. Set the Alignment at Left. On the indents and spacing tabs, set line spacing at "exactly" and At "25pt". On the Line and Page Breaks tab, uncheck all the checkmarks.

Click on Home and set your font style: Courier New 12 or Times New Roman 12. I prefer Courier New 12. It's easier to read.

Follow the submission guidelines of where you're sending your manuscript.

Below is an example of a manuscript format. You can use this if there aren't specific guidelines.

Cover Page
In the top left corner:
Your name
"Writing As" name if you're using a pen name
Address
Phone Numbers (home and cell)
Email Address

In the top right corner opposite your name
Approximate page count.

Eleven spaces down from the top and centered type:

Manuscript Title
By
Your Name (or pen name)

Set up Chapter page:

    10 lines from the top and centered type:
    Chapter 1
    Leave a space
    Begin your story on the next line

Miscellaneous Formatting Tips:

For most publishers use underlines, not italics for anything you want italicized. Check their guidelines. Especially for ebooks. Most ebook publishers want italics, not underlines.

Indent all new paragraphs. Remember in dialogue, each speaker gets their own paragraph.

Use a page break at the end of each chapter. Don't just hit enter to go to the next page. If you do when you print it won't print the way you expect it to. That being said, check with the publisher, E-book Publishers have their own directions for page breaks and how to set up your manuscript.

Many publishers want you to use line breaks or **** for scene changes, especially eBook publishers. Try to make your scene changes smooth so you don't have to use the asterisk. Again, check the guidelines.

If you're submitting by mail -Do NOT use colored paper or ink on a manuscript. Use only white paper and black ink. This same formatting is used for email submissions, but check the guidelines to see if they want the manuscript double or single spaced. It's easy enough to single space it. Just go up to EDIT on the toolbar and click on Select All, then click on Paragraph. Under paragraph on Line Spacing, click on single.

I like to copy and paste my work into a new document before I do this. That way, I always have a properly formatted document to submit to agents and publishers by snail mail.

Click on find and enter each of the words above. These words are passive words, they tell not show. Replace them whenever possible. For ly words, type ly in the find and you'll find every word that has ly in it, but at least you'll find the ones you want to avoid.

Practice Assignment:

Rewrite the story below using everything you learned and Format it for submission to a publisher.

His Right

Leona stood quietly and calmly next to his bed gently stroking his head. Trying not to let her frustration show, she spoke in a soft voice, coaxing him to get up. "Come on Mike, you know it's not good for you to lay here like this

.As usual, he pretended to sleep, his way of ignoring her. Leona understood how painful it was for him to sit in a chair, but she couldn't just let him lay there flat on his back, not moving. All of her training dictated she convince him it was for his own good. He could get pneumonia; and to lie in the same room with the curtains pulled never letting any light in was only going to cause confusion.

He never knew if it was day or night, napping often throughout the day, more from boredom then tiredness. He was a difficult man, not intentionally, but it came so natural. She knew every move was painful and that caused him to be less than pleasant. Sometimes if she even gently touched his knee, he yelled in pain.

Mike was 92 years old and throughout his life had followed orders and done what others expected of him. He led a hard life; nothing came easy. He had worked hard, and supported his family well, raising six children. Wasn't it time to allow him to have his way? To just let him do as he wanted for a change.

What would it hurt to let this poor shriveled up old man eat what and when he wanted, to lay in bed or get up as he chose? Wasn't it time to let him have his way, wasn't it his right?

His children insisted he be kept comfortable and allowed to make his own decisions. If he didn't want to get up or be bothered, he had the right to refuse. If he didn't want his medication, he had the right to refuse that too. He earned him that right, besides nothing was going to change his quality of life, so why insist.

There was nothing wrong with his mind. He was as sharp as a whip. "I have six children, twenty-three grandchildren, and twenty- four great grandchildren." He said proudly.

Everyone thought he exaggerated or made it up, but his family soon set them straight. He was exact in his numbers.

He just wanted to be left alone, and was often irate when they woke him with his meals. He didn't eat them anyway. He just drank milk or ensure and he loved bananas. He insisted he was not allowed to have chocolate.

"I'm allergic to it." He said.

That made his kids laugh. He used to love chocolate. But if that was what he thought then so be it. They didn't argue with him. It was best to humor him. He was happier that way, and that's the way they wanted him.

One or more of them visited every day. On special occasions or weekends they would all come. He was proud of them and he often bragged about them and his grandchildren. He especially enjoyed the visits from the grandchildren with their children. He really loved the little ones. If he got up in his chair at all, it was when they visited. But, he tired easily and often slept trough part of their visit.

He always remembered they had been there though and often told his nurse of their visits, his brown eyes sparkling with a special warmth. He remembered all their names too, although he got a little confused with the youngest great grandchildren.

He had a full head of silvery gray hair and at regular intervals insisted his son cut it for him. His children were ever attentive to his needs and whatever he wanted, they brought. Holidays always brought special food that often went uneaten after a taste

Leona understood he had been an active man and to watch him lay in bed this way bothered her. She tried to convince him to join the others, play a game of checkers, or just socialize. He, of course, refused. He was content to stay in his room, read the paper and occasionally watch television. That seemed to be enough for him. He didn't talk much, even to his roommate. He was a quiet man, unless disturbed.

In the beginning he went to therapy; he seemed to enjoy it and at least was out of his bed and room, talking with people. That ended when they said it wouldn't help, he would not be able to walk again. He had been a tile setter and worked on his knees for 70 years. It took its toll, crippling his knees and back with arthritis.

He often spoke of his wife who he lost two years earlier. He loved her deeply and took the loss very hard. They had been married 62 years and she was his life.

"She took care of me before she died; I didn't even know she was sick. She never complained." He said tearfully. "I didn't even get to say good-bye, suddenly she was gone."

He didn't seem to mind Leona stroking his head this way; in fact he seemed content.

She guessed he would just lie in this position, with the drapes drawn and lights dim until the end.

Mike lived that way for another year, never getting into his chair. Leona never quit trying but more to spend time with him then to convince him. He died late one evening. His daughters were with him at the end and at last, he was at peace. It was his right.

Part 3 – Turning Ideas into Fiction

Lesson 1 – How Much Fact to Put into Fiction

I know well-meaning friends often say -
"You ought to write this down, it would make a
great story."
Well, actually, no it wouldn't. I'm sure
you've all heard the saying "fact is stranger than
fiction" - well it is. If you're writing nonfiction, fine
go ahead and use the story about Uncle Joe getting
stuck on the roof. It was a comical incident and will
make a great creative nonfiction story. However, for
fiction the idea won't make for a great story without
some changes. For the most part, it'll come off as
false. Readers just won't believe it.
Why?
Think about it. Other than Science Fiction -
which still has to be written as believable- when
you read a story or novel, one of your first thoughts
is – can this happen. It might be farfetched but it
can happen. Besides you, the author will be telling
the story. And we want to show our stories.

Here's our incident. Uncle Joe got stuck on
the roof while hanging Christmas lights. He put a
ladder on the peak of the garage and when he went
to get off the other peak he reached his foot out, the
ladder slipped away. He moved toward it and
inched his way off the roof, reached his foot out and
tried to snag the ladder. Again it slipped away. One

more time and it slipped out of reach. By this time he was hanging by his elbows. . No one was in the house. It was cold and the roof was covered with snow. He looked around to see if a neighbor might have come out. Nothing – his arms were getting tired and he didn't know what to do. The only thing left was to jump. He knew if he landed on his feet, they'd slip out from under him and he'd slide off the roof like a bullet. He took a deep breath and let go. Thankfully he landed and didn't slide.

If I were writing it for creative nonfiction, I'd embellish it, make it humorous.

But, how do we create a story from this idea? It almost sounds like an incident from National Lampoon's Christmas Vacation or didn't Grisham do something like this in Skipping Christmas? How did they do it?

Some people need to plot out the idea on paper, which is fine. I wish I could do that. But, I'm one of those writers that just start writing. Oh I'll jot down some ideas and know where I want to go, but in the beginning I usually have no idea how to get there. I know the beginning and the end. What happens in the middle is as much a surprise for me as it is for the reader. And that works for me. Whichever way works for you is fine. There's no absolutes in writing.

Okay, now we have the idea. A man is stuck on a roof. Maybe he's not putting up

Christmas lights. He could be up there for a variety of reasons. Maybe they had a leak and it was raining cats and dogs.

One of the first things, for me, is to start with my characters name, age and appearance. Okay let's call our guy, Charlie. He's middle-aged, slightly balding, but tall and muscular. Next I ask why Charlie was on the roof.

Once I have my characters, I develop my idea. First question: What genre' am I writing? This is where we start asking the questions, what happened, how did it happen, etc. If I'm writing mystery I have to decide is it a murder mystery? Who gets killed, where and why?

Hmm - maybe someone moved the ladder. And maybe Charlie makes it down but he knows someone is trying to kill him. I have a lot of maybes and what ifs.

So, if Charlie is the intended victim we'll need a potential killer.

Once we know the where and why, we need to know if the murder is going to happen in the book, or behind the scenes. In other words has the murder already been committed when we come on the scene or are we going to show our readers the murder. In this case it's an attempted murder because Charlie isn't dead.

Then we need to know how our main character is going to solve the crime. We need some clues, usually not ones the reader will pick up on right away, but clues that at the end of the story they'll hit their foreheads and say "Oh I should have known."

Do you see how we took a real life incident and changed it into something totally different? Sure we could have written humor like National Lampoon, but why stop there. Explore different avenues. You could take the same incident and change it into a romance or fantasy. Maybe even Science Fiction. I don't write that either so I'm not going try to explain it. But who knows maybe while Charlie is repairing the roof, men from mars kidnap him. Let your imagination run wild.

Practice Assignment: Using the incident described above write a story or partial story,

Extra practice: Practice writing fictional stories from every day real life events. Did you witness an accident on the freeway? Change it into fiction, maybe someone ran your main character off the road. Remember ask yourself how, why, what happened.

Write down three amusing things you did or that happened to you.

Example: During the middle of the night, I was startled awake by a loud crash. I raced downstairs and there was a car in the middle of my front porch. (That actually happened to my sister.)

Now write a fictional account of the event. This is just for practice so it doesn't have to be a long story. But I have done this and turned them into long stories.

Lesson 2 - Resources for ideas. – Objective - Finding ideas from everyday sights and sounds.

Everything around us is a potential for story idea. We only have to look at the world around us with a writer's eye.

What do I mean by everything? Here's a good example – Let's say you're stuck in traffic. What do you usually do? Turn up the radio, call someone from your cell phone, and tap the steering wheel impatiently?

Next time turn that negative energy into something positive. Who is in the car next to you, behind you? Is that carload of kids off to a soccer game, Grandma's house? Look at the driver, what is he/she feeling, sitting there with the kids bouncing and jumping around. Her mouth is moving. Is she yelling, singing, playing a game with them. Where are they going? It's a potential story idea.

How about that young couple next to you, are they in love, arguing? Put them in a scene - make up a story. That isn't just a car full of kids, or a young couple. Don't think of it as being stuck in traffic. The same thing applies to standing in line at a supermarket. You're viewing potential characters, ideas, scenes, making up plots. Look in their carts. Are they buying that wine and cheese for a rendezvous or a celebration? A cart full of groceries, three, maybe four gallons of milk, family sized packages of meat, looks like a big family – maybe they take in foster kids. Every place you go you should see potential settings for stories. Everyone you see becomes a potential character.

But let's go a little further -Check out the daily newspaper. Many articles give us ideas for our next plot. Maybe the bank robber will make a good character for our villain. Don't just read the headlines, read the small stories. Read the local pages.

And let's not stop there, look in the classifieds? Under help wanted ads, there are many different and unusual occupations for our characters. Don't skip the business opportunities and legal notices. I found an interesting notice regarding a Public Hearing on the merits of designating several old schools in the area as city landmarks. This piqued my interest since I had attended two of these schools. This could lead to a possible setting for a story or maybe a nonfiction article about a trip down memory lane. Maybe one of these schools is slated to be torn down. It's been vacant for a long time. The crew goes into the abandoned building and finds a body or an old suitcase full of money. See the potential.

Then of course there's equipment. You can learn a lot about a community, especially a small community by what kind of equipment is for sale. A farming community will have a lot of listings for farm tractors or farm equipment.

Don't forget to read the for sale ads. Every conceivable item is for sale from antiques to stereo equipment. I particularly enjoy looking through the jewelry section. One ad for a diamond engagement ring valued at three thousand dollars was listed as a must sell for twelve hundred. The ad raised my curiosity. I figured it was for sale because of a broken engagement. But, what if the woman's husband died leaving her penniless, and she desperately needed money for medical bills. More interesting to me was the thought of who might purchase the ring. I wondered what man would buy a second hand ring, albeit a good deal, for his new fiancée. Then I thought maybe he took it to a jeweler and had it put into a new setting. What would happen, I wondered, if the fiancée found out she had a used diamond. Would she think what an ingenious idea or would she be angry? All this from a one-line ad. The newspaper is an excellent source for ideas.

Magazines are another good source for ideas. Open it to any page, look at the pictures, even the advertisements - we see an attractive woman or a couple. Imagine them in a scene. Create a plot around them. I picked up a magazine the other day and it had an ad for a real estate company. It showed a house with a for sale sign in front of it. It was a beautiful house with a well kept lawn and fabulous landscaping. Why, I wondered is that house for sale? Who are the people selling it? Are their children grown and they no longer need a house this size? Or are they getting a divorce, was there a death in the family? My imagination started to run away with all sorts of ideas about the owners and why they were selling. There are many ways to create stories from simple pictures. Then I began to wonder about the new owners. I wrote a story recently called Shadows in the Attic about new owners who began renovating the attic and found a room. It's amazing how a picture can spark an idea.

But right in your own home you can get ideas. Look around, what do you see? Right now, I see a room with a computer, printer, and a scanner. However, it's not just a room. It's a potential setting for a story. Now lean back and really look at the room. My walls are pewter blue - a cream-colored shade covers the window. If I were writing a story, I would elaborate on this through my character.

Want to turn it into a mystery – try this: Our character, let's call her Evelyn (I have no idea where I came up with that name it just happened, but more about that later.) Evelyn goes to work; she enters her office only to find someone ransacked it. Now through Evelyn we're going to show the office.

Evelyn yawned as she put the key in the lock. Going to have to quit these late nights, fun as they were her body just couldn't take it anymore. She pushed the door open and froze. Her computer lay on the floor and the printer was upside down on the counter. Papers lay scattered over the floor and a purple liquid dripped down the pewter blue walls. Evelyn stifled a scream. The cream-colored shades looked like they were splattered with blood. (Hmm - I may have the beginning of a new story here).

Last, but not least, don't forget your chat room friends or writing buddies. Many times I got an idea for an article just from the conversation. Today the subject of being the only one who managed to fill the ice cube tray came up. One thing led to another and it turned into an idea for a humorous article.

Now let's change it to fiction. Your character bought a bag of ice. When she opened it she found something – maybe a piece of jewelry? How did it get there? We now have the potential for a good mystery. Did someone hide it there figuring on coming to get it later? Was it planted by someone? Where did it come from? Was it stolen?

While creating ideas here are some of the questions to ask. Who, Where, What and Why? Sources for ideas are limitless. We just need to view the world around us with the writer's eye.

Practice Assignment: From any of the ideas I've given above, or one of your own. Write a story or partial story.

Extra Practice: Start taking notes of your surroundings, grocery stores, malls, restaurants. Carry a note pad and jot down the setting, people's actions. Make up stories about them. When you get home write short stories about them. You never know one of them might spark an idea for a novel.

Write a story about snow, a storm, anger, sorrow.

Lesson 3 – Creating Characters from our resources.

Do authors need to lead adventurous, exciting lives like lawyers or doctors to become successful writers?

The answer is a simple, resounding NO!

Can lowly little Charlene Smith, ordinary homemaker, write a best seller? You bet she can! Look at J.K.Rowlings. She actually wrote her novel at a small coffee shop and without a computer. Imagine writing a book in long hand?

However, writers do need excellent imaginations and good ideas. So where do they come up with ideas for their stories?

For starters, write about things you know about and enjoy. Skateboarding, bike riding, hiking, bowling- even working on cars are potential articles or stories. What if a hiker found a dead body? Was it buried in leaves off the beaten path? Why was it there? What happened to it? Was it shot, stabbed, strangled, or did it die of natural causes? You have the potential for a mystery. Or maybe someone brings a car in to a mechanic or body shop. Is there blood on the bumper? Hair strands? Or maybe a beautiful woman brings the car in. The mechanic's attracted to her. Might be the potential for a romance.

One of the first things I do is create my character, usually my main character. I want to know everything possible about them. Not just their appearance and age, I want to know their inner most feelings, their faults and weaknesses. Because without these characteristics, your characters will come across as fake, unbelievable people. I always jot down these important traits. I use index cards, although I have used my character sheets with all the important information listed. Sometimes the index cards work better. They're smaller and can be stored on my desk in a recipe box right next to my computer. How you do it isn't important, that you do it is.

Then I add their occupations. Where were they born? What's their favorite color? Where do they live (town, big city etc)? Do they live in house or apartment? Were they born there? Do they live alone? Do they have hobbies? I have a whole list I go through. These are just some of the questions I ask. I want to know my character like I know myself. Once I know that I can really delve into their personalities. What's their favorite color, likes, dislikes. What makes them happy, sad, angry? But don't stop there it's only the beginning. I want to get into their heads. How would they react to this scenario or that? Is all of this really important? Absolutely, we may not use all of these characteristics in the story, especially a short story, but we know them – that's the important thing. And they are critical for a novel. Get used to doing this. Sometimes these thoughts come to me while I'm cooking or doing the dishes. If I don't think I'll remember, I'll jot them down on a scrap of paper. I've learned the hard way to write them down.

Any character we create may have one of our hobbies or occupations – and how much more believable this character will be because we have first hand knowledge. But that's not the only way to come up with ideas. Now that's not to say you have to limit yourself to these hobbies or occupations. You can always research other occupations and interview people. Maybe your main character is a sheriff or cop. Call your local police department or sheriff's office. They are more than willing to speak with you about their profession. But do have a list of questions beforehand. Don't flail about thinking what to ask. Be prepared. You're taking their valuable time and they're more than willing to answer intelligent questions. At the end of the interview ask if they have anything to add or an interesting story they'd like to share with you, more potential ideas. Libraries are another great resource for learning about occupations, as, of course, is the computer.

Create interesting characters names. Sometimes my character will name themselves I've often started off with a name and as the story continued the name just didn't fit. Silly as it may sound, the character themselves insisted I change it. Another good reason to get into the characters head before you begin.

Characters are all around us. Everyone knows portly Uncle Jess or ample-bosomed Aunt Sophie who can't seem to resist pinching her nieces and nephews cheeks or slobbering them with kisses.

And we all know at least one person who loves to tease and play jokes. Use these characteristics in your stories. (But, please, please remember to change their names and give the other characteristics also.)

We all met a person that no matter how good the news will find something negative about it. Watch people in restaurants, malls, airports. Potential characters are everywhere.

Practice Assignment:. Write a story or partial story creating characters from people you know or have seen.

Extra practice: Write a list of people you know, describe them, add interesting characteristics about them. Now make up a character, combining some of the characteristics if you want, give them names and write a story about them, either using a real life event or an event from the newspaper, magazine, or your imagination.

Write a story about a reunion involving two people who once loved each other but went their separate ways.

Write a story about two people who don't get along and usually avoid each other. Suddenly they're thrown together in a situation where they can't ignore each other (maybe their stuck in an elevator)

Lesson 4 – Learning to Lie – Putting it all together.-

So now we know ideas are all around us - From our workplace to our neighbors. From getting stuck in traffic to grocery shopping and thumbing through magazines to reading the classified, so let's put it all together. You overhear a conversation in a restaurant. The woman is crying. You can't hear the whole conversation. But your writer mind begins to ask questions - Is she breaking up with her date? Is he breaking up with her?

Or maybe those are happy tears? It's not necessary to know the truth. Your writer's mind starts working and you imagine what you want. You begin to formulate a story about it. You begin to build a character in your mind. You can see her clearly. Can even hear his/her voice.

You don't even need to describe the characters in your story as the same description of the people you see. In fact if it's someone you know, it's better not to. We don't want to write about our cranky aunt and have her recognize herself through description. Change her into the complete opposite of what she looks like. Age her, make her younger, but whatever you do don't use her description.

You should create your own characters. Certainly I use people I know. In fact I have a list of friends and relatives with character traits - make one of your own. I add special character traits, like my husband and son have a habit of touching everything on the table and moving it from place to place while you're having a conversation. (Truthfully it drives me up a wall and I often grab their hands to stop them – they don't even realize they're doing it) But that's a trait to add, it makes your characters believable. We all have habits. Some people twirl their hair, some chew on nails. Write them down; use them in your stories.

So, back to our original character, maybe this lady has jet black hair. Your character may have gray hair or blond. Short, long, straight, curly it doesn't matter. What matters is that you create her. Maybe she's young, old, middle-aged. Again, it doesn't matter. Visualize your character in your mind. And make notes!!! As I said previously I use index cards. I list the name of my character, age, color of their hair, height, character traits, who in their family they look like (especially if it's important)

List everything you can to know your character better, even if you aren't going to use it in the story. The more you know about your characters the better and more believable they will be. Nothing is worse than reading about a blond who suddenly has dark hair half way through the story. And be careful with names too. I wrote a story using the character's name, Daniel Stephens. Half way through I changed it to Stephen Daniels. Fortunately, I always ask people to read my stories before I submit them and someone told me about it.

I also use my character work sheets; they include everything from my character's descriptions to their favorite foods and colors. A lot of the information I never use, but that just makes me know my character better. By time I'm done, I feel like she/he's my best friend (or enemy).

And of course the senses, not just what we see, but what we taste, smell, touch, and hear. These senses help your story come alive. Take notes on them too. Become observant. Touch that wood, feel the smooth finish, or the rough texture of a statue. Listen to the sounds around you. Not the everyday sounds of traffic, although those are important too, and sometimes we become so used to them that we don't notice them. But out of the ordinary sounds. Listen to the birds early in the morning or the children playing in a park. These sounds and senses help make your story come alive. Use them.

All of these things combined contribute to good story ideas. Sometimes we come up with an idea from something we touch or smell. Something soft and smooth or a bakery provokes a memory from the past. Use it.

Maybe it's a restaurant, maybe it's a deli or even a car dealership. Take notes on all the places you visit. Settings are often as important as our characters. Write down these settings too, keep a notebook. If a particular restaurant strikes your fancy, take notes. Who knows you may use it someday. I wrote a scene in a restaurant we visited on vacation. It was a quaint little place and I really liked it, so I jotted down some notes and it didn't take long for me to use it. I visited another restaurant with friends and loved the place. It was a typical tearoom type restaurant, definitely for women. It was also an antique store and quilt shop. I just used it a short time ago in a novel. Even hospitals or doctor's office, you never know when you'll have call to use such a setting. Beauty shops and health spas too. Take notes every place you visit.

Which brings me to the last point, find a writing buddy! Someone you can exchange stories with or someone whose judgment you know and trust. Someone you can brainstorm with and toss ideas around. Sometimes we get stuck and just need to discuss the story. They may give you ideas but just talking about it with someone, sometimes gives you the idea on your own.

I strongly suggest finding someone who writes. Only a writer can understand your frustration of a blocked mind or enjoy the feeling of an acceptance. And only another writer is honest enough to tell you what is wrong and right with your story. Often times, family and friends are afraid to criticize your work, afraid they'll hurt your feelings. You want someone honest enough to tell you the strong points in the story as well as the weak points. Trust me, sometimes these critiques do hurt, after all you worked for hours to put these words to paper and you love this story, it's a part of you.

I often ask three people to read my stories. If two of the three comment on the same thing, I know it needs changed. If only one comments on it and the others think its fine, then I leave it. But the end decision is mine to make. It is my story after all.

You want it to be the best you can do, so keep an open mind. If you ask for someone's opinion, respect it. You don't have to take all of their advice, I once had an editor tell me to cut a whole scene. A scene I felt was critical to the story. I had several writer friends read the story. After they were done I asked if they thought I should cut the scene. They all said no, it was too important to the story. Alas, I didn't get the story published, but it remains intact and I've submitted it elsewhere. But I have made changes when an editor suggested them since most editors generally only make suggestions to make the story stronger.

Practice Assignment: Come up with an idea, either from a factual event or your imagination. Create the characters and write the story.

Extra practice:

Think about events from your life and change them into fictional stories, creating interesting characters.

Pick out an item from the newspaper and write your own account of it. Or pick out something from the classified and write a paragraph or two creating a story about it.

Find an interesting occupation. Interview someone or research the occupation and then write a story creating an interesting character with this occupation.

About The Author

Multi-published author, Roseanne Dowell, Writing Instructor and former School Secretary, is an avid reader and writes various types of romance—paranormal, contemporary, women's fiction and mystery. Living in Northeast Ohio with her husband of more than fifty years, she has six grown children, fourteen grandchildren and several great grandchildren. Besides writing, she enjoys quilting and embroidering. Roseanne also enjoys blogging, tweeting, facebooking and posting on various writers blogs. To learn more about Roseanne:

Check her website: www.roseannedowell.com
Or her blog
http://roseannedowellauthor.blogspot.com
on Facebook
https://www.facebook.com/AuthorRoseanneDowell

Roseanne would love to hear from you, email her at rodow62@hotmail.com

Fiction Books By Roseanne Dowell

Secrets, Lies and Love
Designed for Love
Time to Love Again
Shadows in the Attic
Elusive Mission
Deadbeat Dads
Another Day
Geriatric Rebels
Ring Around the Rosy
Trouble Comes in Twos
It's Only Make Believe
All in the Family
Entangled Minds
Love on the Rocks
Two Love Again

www.ingramcontent.com/pod-product-compliance
Lightning Source LLC
Chambersburg PA
CBHW070546290526
45790CB00002B/595